Published in 2012 by
Salmon Poetry
Cliffs of Moher, County Clare, Ireland
Website: www.salmonpoetry.com
Email: info@salmonpoetry.com

ISBN 978-1-907056-96-3

COVER ARTWORK: *Asian elephant*, from James Balog's book *Survivors: A New Vision of Endangered Wildlife*, used by permission of the photographer.
COVER DESIGN: Siobhán Hutson

Acknowledgements

I would like to acknowledge with sincere gratitude the editors of the following journals in which poems in this collection first appeared, sometimes in slightly different form:

American Literary Review	"Pre-Autopsy: Windfall Railway"
The American Poetry Review	"The Hallowed Magician, 1977"
Another Chicago Magazine	"Speak to Me Ushas"
Arizona Attorney Magazine	"Pled"
	"The Day Judge Spencer Learned the Power of Metaphors"
Barrow Street	"Yards"
Chelsea	"Measles (at the Last Minute)"
The Chiron Review	"Ants: The Truer Story"
	"My Men Attorneys"
	"When Academia Took Me to Lunch Then Fed Me the Bull"
Cimarron Review	"Carriage Road and the Sixth Lamentation"
	"Do Not Think for One Minute"
Diner	"Mob Dad"
	"Post-Autopsy: Or, All Those Cell Phones Attached to Your Belt Look like Grenades"
	"Skateland"
Full Circle Journal	"Camping Tips for Singles"
	"Like Bread"
Gulf Coast	"On the Mind Summiting in a Pool of Sweat"
J Journal	"The Persimmon Can See You"
Jewish Women's Literary Annual	"The Dry Cleaner's Daughter"
The Litchfield Review	"Portrait of the Two of You, Festooned"
Square Lake	"Desert Bird"
Smartish Pace	"Bad Boy in Post Office"
The Tusculum Review	"Autopsy: Upon the Tamis Table"
	"Cincinnati Bacon"
Willow Review	"Fossorial"
	"If You See a Naked Attorney in the Ladies' Room"

"The Persimmon Can See You" was nominated for a Pushcart Prize.

"Allotment" and "The Lantern" appear in the international poetry anthology *Not A Muse* (Haven Books).

"Deer" and "The Still" appear in the nature anthology benefiting Habitat for Humanity, *In The Eye* (Thunder Rain Publishing).

"Bad Boy in Post Office" was awarded third prize for the Smartish Pace Beullah Rose Poetry Prize Competition.

"On the Mind Summiting in a Pool of Sweat" was a finalist for the Gulf Coast Poetry Prize.

"Pre-Autopsy: Windfall Railway" was a finalist for the Indiana Review Poetry Prize.

"Fossorial," "The Dry Cleaner's Daughter" and "Yards" appear as part of a chapbook titled *April: Poetry Anthology, Tempe Poetry in April*, Vol. 5.

"Fossorial" was awarded the Willow Review Prize for Poetry.

"If You See a Naked Attorney in the Ladies' Room" was a finalist in the Inkwell Magazine Poetry Competition.

"To the Chief Medical Examiner's Office" was a semi-finalist for the Emily Dickinson Award and appeared in E: *The Emily Dickinson Award Poetry Anthology*.

"Snow Tires at the Auto Garage" was awarded second place in the Chester H. Jones Foundation National Poetry Competition, judged by Robert Creeley, Diane Wakoski and Charles Wright, and appeared in the *National Poetry Competition Anthology*.

"Kafka Can Do" appeared in the *National Poetry Competition Anthology*.

Notes and Dedications

Some of the lines in some of the poems in this collection allude to the extraordinary lyrics and music of Van Morrison. *Sui generis*.

The line "*Is* enough as good as a feast?" in "Do Not Think for One Minute" is paraphrased from the film character, Mary Poppins.

★

"Father-in-Law Sets Right the Troubles with Ceiling Painting" is dedicated to the memory of Annie and Abijah Edlow.

"Passover" is for John Jensen, M.D. and Matthew Bui, M.D., Ph.D.

"Belvedere" is dedicated to the memory of Joseph Holland Chassler.

For their indispensible support of this collection, I am forever thankful to the following individuals, including the exemplary staff of Salmon Poetry Ltd., led by the wondrous Jessie Lendennie; Beckian Fritz Goldberg, Robert Longoni and Deanna Benjamin, two superlative poets and a writer whose editorial insight gave gracious advice on some of the poems in this collection; and to Raymond Renaud, for bringing me to the music, and to Joseph Chassler, in memoriam, for bringing me to the poetry.

For his kindness, decency, wisdom and generosity, I want to express profound thanksgiving for the gentleman Daniel Debrow Edlow. An upright man.

For Daniel

INTERRUPTED QUENCHING

The rapid cooling to a selected temperature by quenching in a suitable medium, holding at the temperature for an appropriate time and then cooling to room temperature to achieve hardness, strength and toughness while minimizing residual stress, the risk of distortion and the likelihood of cracking.

—from MACHINERY'S HANDBOOK

If I ventured in the slipstream
Between the viaducts of your dream
Where immobile steel rims crack
And the ditch in the back roads stop
Could you find me?
Would you kiss-a my eyes?

—VAN MORRISON

Is there—*is* there balm in Gilead?—tell me—tell me, I implore!

—EDGAR ALLAN POE

Contents

I.

AUTOPSY: UPON THE TAMIS TABLE 17

SNOW TIRES AT THE AUTO GARAGE 19

IF YOU SEE A NAKED ATTORNEY IN THE LADIES' ROOM 20

LIKE BREAD 21

DO NOT THINK FOR ONE MINUTE 22

MY MEN ATTORNEYS 24

SPEAK TO ME USHAS 26

SKATELAND 28

BAD BOY IN POST OFFICE 30

WHEN ACADEMIA TOOK ME TO LUNCH THEN FED ME
   THE BULL 32

FOSSORIAL 33

THE HALLOWED MAGICIAN, 1977 34

UP IN TREES 35

THE BIRTHDAY EARRINGS 38

PRE-AUTOPSY: WINDFALL RAILWAY 40

II.

YARDS 43

MIDSUMMER, MIDDAY 45

THE STILL 46

FATHER-IN-LAW SETS RIGHT THE TROUBLES WITH
   CEILING PAINTING 47

CARRIAGE ROAD AND THE SIXTH LAMENTATION 51

MEASLES (AT THE LAST MINUTE) 52

MAN IN BLUE AT CROSSROADS AT CITY PERIMETER 53

WHY THE JUDGE'S CHAMBERS CAN CAN-CAN 54

GEOMETRY FOR INTERMEDIATES   55

CINCINNATI BACON   56

ANTS: THE TRUER STORY   57

PLED   59

HAND ME THOSE GLOVES   60

THE LANTERN   61

DESERT BIRD   62

POST-AUTOPSY: OR, CAN I TAKE JUST THIS WITH ME?   63

III.

PASSOVER   67

CAMPING TIPS FOR SINGLES   69

INTIMATIONS FROM UNDER THE GREAT BEAR   71

THE DRY CLEANER'S DAUGHTER   72

PORTRAIT OF THE TWO OF YOU, FESTOONED   74

MOB DAD   75

KAFKA CAN DO   76

TO THE CHIEF MEDICAL EXAMINER'S OFFICE   77

ALLOTMENT   79

THE DAY JUDGE SPENCER LEARNED THE POWER OF
        METAPHOR   80

DEER   84

THE PERSIMMON CAN SEE YOU   85

BELVEDERE   87

POST-AUTOPSY: OR, ALL THOSE CELL PHONES ATTACHED
        TO YOUR BELT LOOK LIKE GRENADES   89

ON THE MIND SUMMITING IN A POOL OF SWEAT   90

About the Author   93

I

AUTOPSY: UPON THE TAMIS TABLE

The long, leathery, mottled man-luggage
is surrounded. They wheel him in smeared, ungroomed
in the clothes he died in. A festive affair
according to the crease of his trousers.
So the haunt that tapped him tapped him good.
Now a blue gaggle of attendants handles him
roughly. He is icestorm stiff but they
will remove all of it. Wedding band,
modest watch, belt and ornate buckle.
Each is numbered, assigned a clear ziploc bag,
carried away. His otherwise white shirt,
monogrammed at the shirttail, yanked and
twisted off. It is hard to think him dead
with the living swirling about him so, the living
throwing up X-rays, taking his fingerprints,
photographing him, aerial view
from the top of a ladder, and crude to stare
at his nakedness. Gentler instead to think of the tussle
the attendants have with his wardrobe: how like the bygone days
of a mud-spattered four-year-old, toy trucks clutched in each hand,
called in from play, surly, resistant to the taking
off of his clothes. Tantrum half a minute
away.

Because a severed carotid artery cannot
be speckled-pupped away.
Because some dark fugue repeats
in the background. The chief wanted it;
the attendants cannot rumble about it.
The perforated tamis table the man-luggage
rests on oozes his ruddy
fluids into a trough-like basin beneath.
Sterilization doesn't dwell here. Hardware store
pruning shears crack the rib cage
wide open, cuticles of meat stuck

still to the blades. Organs and fat the mystic
clothing he'd packed for his autarkic spree,
here now spread out, circling the terrible hole
of his middle. Kidney socks balled in
on themselves from spatial concerns, cushioned
in fat like pastries. Stomach a dress shirt
folded over then under to lessen
wrinkles. Cropped runt of a left lung
obliging the muscle of all muscles. Endless
astonishing intestine, like the champagne
ruffled skirting around a buffet table.
Burgundy liver, sleek tuxedo shoes
in a shiny bag. Esophagus
a bouquet of glossy pearls. Two or three
globular mysteries, pomegranates
packed for snacks. Peachy
pomegranates. Delicious looking. Soft as heaven.

It happens again today, and tomorrow it will:
The amber-stained cutting board. The old scalpel,
fluted knife, expert hands uttering for the dead.
A restaurant ladle scoops up pooled
blood in the rib cage cavity,
adventive punch bowl at the big
family reunion. Slop bucket
below the table lined with a plastic garbage bag.
The parts of a man sliced and thrown in.
Far away, a bass note fastens the room, long bow
easing over strings for a small forever.
Enter the angels of all our minds.
Before the curly fish needle
pulls him together, the bag is twisted once,
twice, heaved out of the bucket and plopped
down into his middle. Garbage bag and all.
Hey man, here's your stuff back—
Don't think we took anything much, really—

SNOW TIRES AT THE AUTO GARAGE

How different I am, for the third time,
how changed. I know what he likes
is the long earrings. The raccoon
collar around the coat. These appliances.
The way I don't stir around as much. He likes that
I just stand there, and talk, like a mute person.
Being pleasant is how ladies act. Twisters are not pleasant.
I ask questions he loves to answer. How's the wife,
how's the new baby. He is a working man.
A nice man. But he does not attend.
I can tell I am hardly there.
I have confided much to him in the past. Not once
has he revealed my secrets.
What I wish I could do, if doing makes matter,
is take him over to where he can hear
and disrobe: Now this, this is just an act.
I'm still the same girl with the same things.
It's only that I've learned now when to
release myself and when to contain myself,
that's all. It's none of my business really.
The act is a table I tolerate.
I hate it even.

IF YOU SEE A NAKED ATTORNEY
IN THE LADIES' ROOM

Don't tell George. Did we not have one god-awful time
getting order restored the day the racist cookies were solicited in?
His desires to see and not to see are wholly construction,
a ritual laxity of his covenant, and he sees despite himself,
spiralling bombardier in the drapery folds of his mind—
the imported wool court suit in a sienna heap
like a deposed flag on the tile floor. The makeup
wands and color pots strewn across sink and counter.
Her prismatic earrings casting lyrical, bewitching light
upon and beyond the winking mirror. The woman herself—
bony, freckled chest, breasts the size of hardened
limes, the mystifyingly long, middle-aged hair. And too,
her studied holding of the precisely chosen pen,
its cloisonné entrapment, taking the measure of herself.
Only the earrings left on, and the high-heeled slingbacks
to lift the buttocks like the hindquarters of a doe,
anatomical hammers, with the hint of the fleecy comical, as
in the vigorous moment the creature forefeels, peers
through the leaves of the poplar trees, down
the black ravine, short snorting of the nostrils, the turn
toward, turning back, furious flee from
the undetectable blued barrel.

The naked attorney with relish says no man will demur her charms.
She cocks one pale, diminutive hip, accentuating pelvic
bone, its shallow hollow. In any social room every fellow
has his want, but her heart's longing not to be trod upon
binds their poor folly so that they end rapturously, loathing her.
And she wonders why the church wives shoot
her nasty glances. Would you tell her something
stamped black confidential arrived from the bar association,
the meter is expiring, and the loutish python has once again
escaped in her young son's room at home. Coiled around
around and around one pine bedpost, it lazes
indifferent to the brutal mess downstairs.
The boy cannot retrieve his books for school.

LIKE BREAD

As marksman. As target. As one teething a chalcedony-ringed rule
of thumb: go small, target, small as an infant's toenail set in
the jaws of vernier calipers. Veil what you value. But no—
a target must unfurl, be slyboots, go big as the cirrus-stripped sky.

Time renders unutterably. More than a few missed deadlines
is no stasis. The tirade on rickety wheels is just that; let nothing
bear reference to critical, save health. At the decorative object,

males throw; they pick up to throw. Females pick up to pocket.
Worlds whirl on such sleuthing. Across the proverbial valley—
Stampede. Could be good. Could be crisis.

Like bread, slow rise
helps develop character.

The animal makes new every day
his catch.

Man supplements.

that because she is having a nervous breakdown
and because the two of you are in an empty field
and she is arranging a string of multicolored
pennants in a tremendous circle
and you are getting paid to watch her do this
that you are any less a decent and upstanding person
for the weirdness of this transaction.
She agreed to your services at your rate;
you assumed that would involve the legal usuals.
You came to draft on behalf of strangers.
Once, singlehandedly, she protected
all the employees of her state, afforded
them the luxury of composure
in their employer's house. Fame found her
when a nurse client refused to bare her buttocks
during an office canoe-trip mooning incident.
How could you possibly know she would
arrange these flags on the grass in a circle
and bandy around within, wingless
but away, away?

Just know that even this is not the subversion.
Odds being what they are, there still
was that fresh patio umbrella, anonymously
cranked wide open in the low visibility dust-and-grit
windstorm, not wise you say, the significant damage
to the fabric, the frame twisting, but wait. The umbrella
lifted straight up, out from its metal stand—like Mary
Poppins swelling over the slanted English rooftops—
only to collapse, plummet savagely back to earth.
But not earth precisely. Rather the velvety
pleasant-smelling head of the toddler
being jogged in the stroller by his mother
increasingly frantic to escape the eyeless storm,

impaling itself in the child's
crown with the nonchalance of a lottery winner
one year past payday. There's your bad news kiddo.
Is enough as good as a feast?
Ask that of the physician, who in the operation
to remove, must elect
between language and ambulation.

MY MEN ATTORNEYS

The woman attorney smells better. She'd like to
believe she can't help it but it's useless, and she won't;
in her book, the legal term *deliberation* is an act of loss.
One whiff resoundingly weeds out charlatan, crusader,
the judicial truffle. Allow that she is nutty as a holiday
cake, for rise she will to your infernal occasion
to purge and catapult you from the crazy-
tongued mouth of your intimate bespectacled dragon.
The woman is granite, and bronze, come from
the lost wax method. My men attorneys
are craven. And they built an industry on it.

Over the telephone a favorite law office sings "Happy Birthday."
Even the young associate of bad faith, at the elder
partner's urging, participates. After it's sung, the learned man
hears, "Thank you from the bottom of my heart," — and he erects,
"She said 'Thank you,' and something about her bottom."
It isn't the sexual titillation; it's beneath it, where the
lips fancy the sugared foil's undoing, *ex parte*.

A woman arrives for the interview.
Her life is hers; the two preschool kids, the busted
fuel pump in the car, the bills. All she's come for is the job.
After the attorney tells her about the hours and his practice
and his pay scale he actually says:
I need somebody to tell me
with a straight face that my priorities
come before theirs.
What is stunning in the captious air before her dumb rejoinder
is why his only true friend, when he was seven, was imaginary.

Another attorney says excitedly,
in front of the father of the deceased teenage boy,
This is the case I'll retire on, I'll make so much.

Can he help it? His analyst would conclude
the fourth-grade locked them all in: when the teacher
called the plain girl up to pass out tests, he scrutinized her,
her unformed hands, thumbing the papers, counting the
people per row, number of tests needed, take one
and pass it back, he watched her with wet eyes, she
might have thought he liked her, a small crush, the real boy,
her heart jumped, but he hardly saw her, *he wanted that test.*
The test is him; the girl, an addendum, otherwhere.

SPEAK TO ME USHAS

Do I like feeling sick?
Even the best of cults ages peevishly.
To your mother's face I have frequently
called you an obsequious child. My
dearest friend, she understands, has patience,
knows coercion, is married to a fair man in psychiatry.
Lovely couple, your mother, your stepfather. This,
she has screened this, phase four, Ushas' adulting
posturing, she finds all this what she calls enchanting,
always pleased to see me frustrated, I'm up to my ears in
stained glass gew-gaws and she says you'll grow
out of it. How many years have I known you? Since you were
born, yes. Fifteen years you've been at bay, your grubby
kid's hands, I'm unqualified
to teach, speaking to show only what has been shown me
but you're continually here now, me your mother's friend,
side pressing your boyish hip against my anatomy.
Lately you call me "this year's woman," my pretty
curves, you follow. What could these mean, I'm sorry
about these tokens you bring, bugle-beaded pouches and
tigers' teeth, what are they, obviously
unlawful to say nothing of useless,
absolutely unlike those a smiling graybeard once brought
your mother, who as a young girl herself,
sixteen years old with darts
on her blouse, all in a modest tizzy
thanking, hoping him a good day, never to expect
the consequences of such meeting, a large part of which
presents me now with charms I hardly deserve.
How does one bed down a child anyway, they never talk
when they should, and they wait on signals
they then pathetically screw up. Children want a harmless tango.
You, Ushas, your mother trusts my discretion;
she loves me. You take so after her, nobody's a fiend.

Just if I only had some pamphlet, or I should keep
or should I keep from praying get the hell off, go
easily for once, don't make pictures of me, find your own friends.
I'm lazy. In pain to boot. Everything is due
and nothing is done, keeping now, what's next, from the
numbing singular gape
of your fine black eyes at my open throat, like a vampire's.

SKATELAND

I had to be pretty old when I finally got that my mother
hadn't taught me proper hygiene. Sixth grade. Training
bras. Yes, you washed them but who knew
how often. Marcy Goldman washed hers every
other day. Weeks I went. She had all the Nancy Drew
mystery books. I had the same volumes on my shelves
but she read hers.

That afternoon the walkway smelled
of cement; everything so saturated it all
but gurgled. Maple trees slung sodden arms
down to their sides in tree fatigue. We three sat on
backyard cushions on the front step of Marcy's house.
Swatches of something lay scattered on the pavement
where the private walk turned common. Wet
from rain, grainy, greenish-hued, torn-out magazine pages,
they stuck as if glued to the path. Overgrown
untended bushes. High grass. Kids. Boys,
7- or 8-year olds, in some kind of back country yard
or edge of the wood. They stood completely naked
in almost Pre-Raphaelite poses, their little flaccid penises, scrotums
like wilted roses. Doughy forms. One boy holding the tip
of the branch from a bush as if for
balance or from modesty.

And he was certainly a boy, but I, eleven-years-old,
shunned interest in a boy-child's nudity. I fancied Paul Revere
and the Raiders, The Rascals, grown rock-and-rollers,
hullabaloo summery, just dangerous enough to put me down
wildly but stop when I said stop. If they listened; if I cried.
Grown men who'd mastered the excrescence
of the erection, a function which eluded my sixth grade
mind, made me feel unpicked. Paul Revere's penis
would've discovered a painful resistance to

its knocking, my hymen a tight drum skin then. If only Paul
had moved up—there he'd have found an itching supplicant.
Way back at seven I'd discovered
it, or rather, my Ken doll discovered it. Not sure
how he got there, but there he got he did, found it with his feet.

I do not know how long I stood motionless
at the walkway near the curb
but I could not tear myself away from the look
of strain on these boys' faces, as if what they knew
was this was stupid, or foolishness, and what was the point of this,
this ugly thing with no point to it—and a feeling came upon me
of being watched while I peered at these things,
someone from behind some window curtain
stroking some part of themselves. Hoping
for a reaction maybe. I'm talking about a form
of destination. Shame tapped me, followed by a weird aroused
repulsion, and I tried to discard them,
the torn-off pages, I shook and shook my hands
to release me from them.

BAD BOY IN POST OFFICE

The bad boy is a contortionist, sits face cheek
to wood, bottom in the air. It must be nice-feeling
because he stays that way a long while.
Post office bench for the elderly or infirm
or seasonal people with giant holiday boxes.
He yells, to his mother standing first in line, *see him!*
Porter his name is, with instructions
to get down immediately. But like an astronaut
in slo-mo and black space, he's all mystic antennae,
as if in wonder about his own body, what it
answers to, how it acknowledges.
From that angle anyway, the peculiarity of the
post office's whole world.

I suffer in line with my own stack of critical mail.
Ahead of me a patient tidily-dressed woman shakes
her head. She chuckles like bubbles. Porter says,
"That lady's hat is big," meaning me, and my 8-inch-brim
gambler-style straw. His mother, preoccupied
with the bottom of her handbag, searches for
that darned Up escalator. Doesn't everyone have
a full-size moving escalator in their pocketbook?

Porter slides alongside the postal clerk counter,
jiggles the doorknob of a locked door. Grunts
to pull it open, both hands clawed around the knob. Leans
his foot up at the base for more leverage, kid version
of conflict of interest. At sea at the foot of a silver
escalator in Nordstrom is Mom. And then he grabs
hold of, throws down a cardboard stand-up
advertisement for post office paraphernalia,
maybe five feet high. Stamps
on top of it in sparkly blue fish sandals.

I hate him. The tidy woman glances my way.
"Well, we were like that once, too" she says. I say
"I don't think so" and she says "Yes we were all that child" and I say
"No ma'am, we were not" and she says "Well yes, but that was
us, back in the day." Yes, back in the discontinued day, when
a kid preferred a full set of teeth for life. If you only *thought*
a thing, from out the very corner of her eye
your mother could yank you by the hair
without laying on a finger. No talking back
or about it and no mumbling
or trouble would brew worse
than the thing you simply thought about.
The woman says confidentially, her grandmother
always told her she could hear so well a mouse
pissing on cotton boomed like a foghorn.
And we laugh together, loudly, for our done
childhoods, for their candid memory-lit roads, roads
gone under water or overgrown with crabgrass
or paved slick and shiny in asphalt or concrete
but we laugh anyway and for all the bladder-filled
mice of the world
and for the flood that wrecks disdain.

WHEN ACADEMIA TOOK ME TO LUNCH
THEN FED ME THE BULL

Been out on the patio all morning reading the great
humanist poet David Kirby between
glasses of iced orange pekoe tea. The poem
about Mr. Polanski's directorial distractions
with his wanted cookies
bent me over with one of those soundless
gaping-mouth laughs from which I experienced
the elation of the perfect moment,
where, if I were now dying, I was too happy not to embrace it too.
When the noise of laughter finally
caught up to my body's visceral take on it,
the dogs three houses down barked rabidly and made
altogether threatening wolf sounds in my direction. Bitches!
Naturally, this triumphal rise brought out the old, phobic
black-garbed, misanthropic graduate student in me.
A kind of papyrus pang verging on ogre-
tinkering leapt off the bookshelf.
Vilely I switch-hit, and read some poems
of _____'s. Ninety-nine
viscid summer days it seemed,
on my delicate hands and delicate knees
scrubbing
the feculent tile floor of a big-city airport,
its air-conditioning broken, its
gift shops locked and barred.
Now, I like
astringent, biconcave, crib biting,
obscure reference-relating, foreign
tongue-spewing poetry
as much as the next guy.
But there is something to be said
about a poem on a page
you can turn to and just deliciously imbibe.
Let the succor mercerize your tongue.
It's not as if the flatware has to match
for the dining to be cuisine.

FOSSORIAL

The day before my older brother turned three
a mass of gray clouds swept down the north
corridor, unprovocative mitten of Wisconsin, railing
into Chicago like a runaway train. Snow fell mad
in a vertiginous trance deep into night
where a wind took up off that magnificent lake
throwing snow drifts, six forbidding feet high,
against the front doors of east-facing houses. To unlock
the entrance hailed an avalanche.
Shonie and Morrie Stein could not make it. Bob
and Gloria Weisberg would not. And the ballroom dance
lessons my parents signed on with them
—cancelled. The dance studio roof
caved in, a névé collapse, the compacted snow brutish
and unreceptive to the tentative arts. But the birthday dinner,
fashioned for these adult friends, went on.
Deficient, the serving utensils against such presentation.
Atop doily'd platters, cheddar chutney canapés
berthed between Parmesan artichoke hearts.
Turkey tetrazzini calorific in its silver-domed
chafing dish; underneath, small warming votives
flickering like whispers. The centerpiece
a pretty chocolate torte, candleless
beside a gravy boat brinked with raspberry sauce.
My family ate. My mother opened my brother's gifts.
Red drum. Cowboy hat brimmed in leather stitching.
A shiny brown hobbyhorse; my brother hugging it.
After they tucked him in bed it was my father
who turned, touched the bracelet at my mother's wrist.
Suggested some refreshment. A gentling daughter. Contingency.
He must have known I would climb out of that house,
a delving spade and the book of seasons strapped upon my back.
His thick tame hand guided my mother into my life.

THE HALLOWED MAGICIAN, 1977

for Joseph Chassler

> *"We certainly couldn't say*
> *the same thing about rocks."*

Then there's one who's earnest, who echoes Plato first
and Robbe-Grillet second,
and if God hadn't made him a man
he would have been, what? heresy, plague,
herbs, poultice, health, property.
A disc humming in fierce velocity,
soundly, its shadow behind, likelihood ahead.
Here as they say, twisted and jaded as memories go,
what appears is what wants to appear: Resonant, irritable hands,
the wafting scent of dubious conceit, nice thin legs.
He thinks covering himself with jipijapa leaves
and jacks-in-the-pulpit will distract me from my schoolish excuse.
So what if I could kill him. Kill him or be him.
Fumes climb from him like theatrical devices. Out of his head
he grows Einstein's negligence cut,
below which inherited eyebrows collide, twin nightwalkers
in happy mime. But especially his eyes. Narcotic.
Bloody true, they say, give it up, you're a baby,
do something for yourself, insanely,
wracking my skull into bits, from the eyes
comes the calling: Some carpenter, the hallowed magician,
he sways on the podium under limelight, unleashed
in a fixed cast, neglecting his applauding audience.
What diffidence! What a pretty boy!
And the dynamic rite, cutthroat and bruising, comes at leisure,
twining around and enters, it knows the impossible
and splices me back like a carcass revived from the spoil.
Bloody well then, you made it, have at it. Vanity,
incalculable error. Artfully, none else exist for him,
flicking cranial bone chips off his lapel,
he is something strange and worth it:
a spirit unpossessed by steel or salt
a spirit laughing and cursing in a water bath.

UP IN TREES

For the Trees

Anyone's guess why the man and woman
fighting in the backyard of the house across
do not care that they are heard. Or
why their argument, giant gila monster
flicking a pink-forked tongue long
as an airplane runway, panics me, an uninvolved.
What exactly do the experts mean by upbringing?
And why should I turn indoors anyway? Isn't the gorgeous
scent of the shadowy tall cedar mine
to uptake? Hundreds of spindly needles worrying
the ground. What of the Inca doves plucking
up the new rye seed, reducing probable grass
to bird feed in one fell swoop? The citrus blossoms have
fallen like a wedding veil, exposing their fruit. I half-expect
gunshot to hailstone into my yard.
     "Why can't you be a good woman?"
"I want to be a good woman. I want a
regular house. Sheets for shades, Chester,
it's disgusting. Since when is a wall clock
a luxury? Back up man,
you best bounce."
     "Pack your shit and get out."
The soft whistle is my dog's favorite. I want him in.
If they offend his brown fur head I think
I must pull the shotgun from under
the master bed. And won't that be pretty
bad six o'clock news footage? My physiology
absorbs their vitriol; to expel it
something more potent than hurling dog feces
into that yard close to midnight is warranted. People,
the sign on the box says second-hand smoke
sickens without consent. I can read. You can read.

The Forest

Out in the temporal world, they make judges
to cope with the damage of disenchanted twosomes
and this judge likes to get a rhythm going,
is prone to off-the-cuff dramaturgy, so
would prefer himself high
upon a craggy, moody cliff, beneath a stewing
overcast sky, as in a heavily-draped Brontë tome, a
cloaked man, a raven man, a man of prevenience
and says to mother and father: *hatchets! you'll be up*
in trees yourselves. You'll be under cars, you'll be at it
with small cameras in large arenas, looking
to hoist a disparaging rock in the direction
of the unbeloved. You'll
be sitting around thinking up ways
you can show me *where the other person*
is violating one of my orders.
Summoned to fracases, men like this, for whom
the refrain, *not more of the same*
but more of the like, is the elevation their ear requires,
the woven story traveled backward—
as pioneers in covered wagons come to a place
of sunder, of scorched earth—had this ground been trod
once in joy, had it shimmered under the brilliant
sun in undulating fields of blue-eyed grasses? Look down yourself,
the precipice is steep, not for the faint, for a man
to be asked to cleanse the eye of quandary: whether
to purge the rancorous giant
swallowtail caterpillar from off the navel
orange tree, caterpillar mimicking a snake
covered in bird dropping, uncomely, designed
to survive through cunning ugly camouflage,
caterpillar nothing but hungry and wanting to live,
can't help how it looks, or what it feeds on—
parentage's menu. But the orange tree
has other needs and preserving its leaves

is one of them. To make oranges
from nothing is full-strength, knotty business.
Yet the butterfly born caterpillar, if it can early on
sidestep the garbage pail, will be elegant.
Black and yellow-spotted flutterer, intricate banner alive.
Whose interests then does the raven man parlay
into a burst of finale? Orange or butterfly.

THE BIRTHDAY EARRINGS

You are a grown woman now but
back when you were a teenage girl
you went to bed for the first time
with a man now also a woman. Full-size. Sharply
built. All the parts-and-pieces.
A sex change operation, the flagrant kind, and
according to old neighborhood hens, quite attractive,

as a Las Vegas showgirl is striking.
You remember a thickish oyster-colored biker
with ugly glasses, hands like soft mitts and
an intense thing for Ann-Margret.
You liked the Harley best, but not stuck on the back of it
getting drenched in the shifting rain. Behind foggy
rolled-up car windows, people smirked.

In the basement of his parents' home
he squirted liquid butter on sandwiches, made you
call his boss and say he was sick, had sex
without really penetrating anything, clumsy,
oafishly, but you were young. You never
wanted sex in the first place. You wanted
just to be held.

For your birthday, he presented gold-tone
hoop earrings, and both earlobes rashed.
On that last Friday night he phoned: you'd better
be in a dress. You ran the half-block
to your best friend's house, afraid, thrillingly, that he was nuts,
that he might do something with all those biker chains.
He must've rung your bell over and over

while you and your friend opened fortune cookies
in her bedroom. Printed on your paper slip: *You will stumble
into the happiness of your life.* And so into the bracing
late autumn night she and her dad walked
you home. There was the proper smell of cold bare
maple trees. Promise of winter's crystallization.
The congested, sleeping street—it whispered

to you, halo-lit by streetlamps, a street you knew better
than any one person—the considerable times you walked it
from someplace you shouldn't have been or someone
into whose hands you insinuated your temporary curiosity.
No one but the cat was home. The cat was foxy
and smart, had learned how to tip the ringing
phone from its cradle, and before that

had learned if the phone began its ring and she
in your lap, out she'd jump to give you way.
Thankfully, the fancies of twisting the front door knob
she'd not yet finessed, but not for lack of the most ardent trying.
She mothered ten kittens.
Oh, she tried so hard to reach you
and she was your friend for the longest time.

PRE-AUTOPSY: WINDFALL RAILWAY

Substantial wall of scenic frosted glass—
glittering soft hills, traveler in silhouette, staff in hand,

head tilted in the direction of a hunch. Mountain pass
way in the distance, locomotive surfacing upward. Past the wall—

a plain door. Window in it, size of a postcard. The receiving room.
Cold, slender, and more daredevil than any sheer

rock face on earth. Blue or white zippered bags. Surnames
sprawled across in black marker. Garden flock stacked

against the unadorned walls. All else, metal, frozen—
the multi-tiered rolling bunk racks. Such lull of chamber music

squeezing from the refrigerator compressor. A dangling chord—

drifts down to the long married couple, at ease, out
for a gala evening. Both were nothing if not urgently missed.

His unlittered billfold lay in the gutter beside the crushed
beaver top hat, a thing he once dismissed as ridiculous.

Days-old theater tickets expelled from the dropped
beaded bulb of a bag. Rather

to enter a sleeper car on the lux arctic train, nightrobe of heavy
garnet velvet, smoking jacket quilted, belted, lushly lapeled.

Faraway folks we anticipate will be comfortably good
to go, just a soft drag into the wenge-paneled, fancy-ceiling'd

twinkling station. Someone offer a toast
to the scalpel. It shirks the hurrah

of living flesh beneath the well-nourished cardigan.

II

YARDS

I

That a wife came with the old world
baggage of her mother before her, and
that babies would grow up to be people
so they needed to be prepared for it, and
there had to be a common language in a family,
not a family of babel, of glass doorknobs and
back porch lights, and of unshared meals.
Not that he didn't love his family
but he didn't know what to do with it.

II

Meander around to that place
where you set foot to ground that
cultivated you. That ache in your heart
for the past is natural.
It's the desire, and the failure
of desire, to move
the misshapen forward.

III

Beneath spring's yellow-fingered forsythia
the little wrens and turtles wrapped in handkerchiefs,
buried tenderly in shoeboxes,
have gone to earth.
At the fenceline, rosebushes
rupture with soft purposeful buds of enchanting color.
Someone—impossible for you in all ways
but one golden one—will knock; have inviolate recognition. Await
the curative. The trees bear food.

IV

And so the pear is good fruit. Try the pear;
why not the pear *and* the dark, picked cherries? The
nutritive day crows with chance. Cleave without rue.
When your person approaches the entranceway,
like the brilliant dog, perpetually awash
in jubilant earnest,
ridiculously bound to him.

MIDSUMMER, MIDDAY

The crickets have not
yet decided they want
indoors. The Bermuda grass
tentacles toward the arcadia door,
waxy tough spikes. The creatures
outside sense, but do not yet know
the oppression the heat
promises. Everything
acts as if great
slabs of time were its entitlement. The brown dog
gnaws on pigs' knees from
the boiling pot of collard greens. He
is elated. The sky looks slow and blue.
A parcel was delivered
but the house is uncomfortable
and the surprise can wait.
Hey, Dan, did you ever
fix that lawnmower?

THE STILL

Big city girl in Virginia woodland to prove a point.
Anyone could be friends with nature—
I was there to try to see what
he saw. Between the trees, the stillness,
the steep drop to the ravine. Rain had passed
and washed color from the timber,
the sky sullied thick with gray.
I was not to worry my hair
would frizzle up past recognition. I'd been brought
to his favorite backdrop, and was being courted.
But because in any kind of place
I search for the aberrant thing, the corner
of my eye caught the red tail
of the arrow poking up through the
deep pliant floor of leaves,
and I was not surprised I'd found it.
In me it created a noise of danger
but the woods were immune, the woods
I was told, would embrace it like a brooch.

FATHER-IN-LAW SETS RIGHT THE
TROUBLES WITH CEILING PAINTING

So long as each piece does its work
the arch is alive, singing, a restless choral.

　　—CARL SANDBURG

Ribbons of River

I was delivered by airplane to the tidewaters of Virginia
to face the family of my betrothed.
Looked at from above the place was a dream tapestry, bunches
of dense green treetops tied up by silver ribbons of river.
And why hadn't I paid attention in seventh grade
history class? Down at ground level every patch of
dirt and field of grass was significant. Each plot supported
a plaque affixed by a stake: here bloody colonists rallied
for a baby America. The grass and ground
exclaimed their passing. Surrender Field flew past my rental
car window and I thought hard about surrender.
Not two miles from the home I approached, in a now dozy field,
Cornwallis, mortified in defeat, handed his true sword
over to the enemy. Myself a wreck. The need so big
to be consented to.

I spent the week withstanding trial by curious stranger.
The seventh day finally my lover flew in. His father and I
took the old blue truck to the airport. Perfect time I thought
to ask the question that might expose
his mind, get to the heart of his working.
Had he a happiest time? Myself nearly a newlywed,
I thought he'd easily say his own wedding, the births
of his children. Or retirement, or his vegetable garden.
So when I heard him say the army, during the war, I was dumbfounded.
When would it ever be about me?

Orbit of the Project

The Italian countryside and road to Rome
were sleek postcards. Young men in Army uniform,
there for no reason but war, bearing rifles in World
War II Italy, did not ring any bells for the relevance
of architecture. Still, Abijah had known church.
The chicken-raising, Virginia boy knew of the frescoes
the Sistine Chapel housed, that a man spent years
in the concave bends of a whorled ceiling, with exquisite
distractions, rotting feet, behind schedule, full of touched
vision. The scaffolding alone a web of increments.

He let his eyes drink up the yellow angled light
that hung like smoke in the gallery. His mates
in uniform, their heads tilted back, their mouths agape
from the orbit of the project, the fresh army boys
and ceiling together seemed, while he could not name it,
a kind of majesty. And so Abijah
fell to the scrutiny of the lesser panels—
the Libyan Sibyl with her contorted left toe, the
spherical right arch. A book she had the mind
to lift surely was an atlas of the cosmos, its bearing
so large some crane was required, or a kind friend
with a knowledge of levers. No help from the
flummoxed angels beside her; they were consumed
with euphuism and the pointing skills of the underappreciated.

In a small slow circle Abijah took in
the soot-laden, lime- and plaster-crackled ceiling.
One wall panel cradled the learned man Zechariah. Underneath
the folds of gold fabric in the man's robe, Abijah could see,
rimmed with dusk, an arbor of fat black grapes
traced vine upon arched vine, a prediction of wine.
And again, up above, in a starring fresco, the new idea
of light made darkness a firmament. At the fresco's
border, a reclining nude, dull rose scarf twisted

around his head, geared to reveal rasps of wire whisk and leather
bolts to fasten brushes. Jehovah's
right armpit held the profile of the artist's pet goat.
And so on the paper sack that held his lunch, Abijah drew
a simple pump, a contrivance to drive solvents up there, that a
vision might lift up from a vision, and he left
the drawing propped at the baseboard. What a house was this?
The sensation of hurtling backward and throughward
occupying one space.

Women Long Down

Back home the sun had broken, was climbing, coaxing
the tops of the collard greens in his mother's
garden to splay outward, lushly verdant. Country birds
called from the deep of the massive poplar tree.
His girl, Annie, north in Philadelphia, had been up
long before dawn, rushing to catch the first trolley,
deliver her to her domestic work. There was Annie
to court and satisfy, and persuade to leave the city,
come down to York County with its gravelly bowed
roads and blackberry bushes. Boys to be
made and reared, last boy born to carry the strange
name of the quiet soldier Abijah had befriended
in war, and distant women long long down the road
for those boys to be men with, go toe-to-toe with, everyone
all the more glad for the science of it.

The Boy Will Be

The county had finally flattened and paved
that dangerous road. No one was particularly thrilled.
It hummed briskly with traveling passers-by.
My husband and I returned to Virginia to bury
his mother, the woman who called herself
Hard Rock Charlie, yet bought for my husband, unreluctantly

when he was a small child, a doll-baby with yellow
string braids, which he would not let go of
in the store, bought because it was a thing he'd be tender to,
said the saleslady to his mother, the boy
will be tender. The year we married
his mother told me that story, opened a
dresser drawer in the spare room, brought out
the old yellow-haired doll. I wanted to ask for it
but I could see in her eyes her son in the making.
And so on and on until I found myself standing in blue
on the back stoop of the house my father-in-law built
from the ground up. I watched and thought
about the three-foot long black snake the brothers
trapped in the driveway beside the funeral limousine.
His mother, like me, had feared snakes. My husband
and his brothers talked about it a little, calm and unamazed.
Someone was going to move it in a metal bucket
to the deep woods out off the field. Someone else
said to just run it over with the car. They all laughed
softly at that, a thing they would not do.

CARRIAGE ROAD AND THE
SIXTH LAMENTATION

Julia. The uniformed schoolboy with the flag at the gate
intuits nothing of crinoline and Kentucky, and covetous beaus.
But to turn on a child out of nowhere. It was
that ghoul in the wood, the wood embracing the inn,
his bloated paunch all you remember of him, the dank, weed-ash wood
where he repeatedly violated you until you went blank,
conscious but blank, you could not detect yourself
but sorely heard the scratchings of beetles and crickets along
the ground, the riffle of foliage, airplane engines
rumbling overhead. Somewhere you heard your daddy
call, *Julia*, his dreamy voice, *let's eat at Meck's,*
Julia, come on now, where long past closing, he brought you.
You ate and then rifled the empty maroon booths for change
from patrons' pockets, returned to table with coins
cupped in your small hands, your shining eyes.
You knew this did not belong to you, and
there
you distinguished him
square before you, he bent slowly, came forward, and
you left, you closed your eyes, you had to, you loosened to die,
not in time to glimpse his hand wrench into a fist and with
his yellow words *"have it your way,"* down came all his
force against the whole of your turned cheek,
cracked your jaw in two like a canary bone. Months
clenched in a brace, you shunned regimen. Time lost you,
a black boneless wound. That is why
today, you at the outside driveway, walking your grounds,
come to the formal wrought-iron exit and shudder to see a boy.
He speaks to you, is asking something, and since you are gone
to the scene behind him, you mistake several cars for blocks
or boulders or birds on wing, and since you hate
children and fear words, you glare at him.
There is nothing else but the constellation of night luster
coming on, and the billowing smoke swelling out
your highest chimney, in it, only ash, no retribution, no
restitution, no frank and revivifying cessation.

MEASLES (AT THE LAST MINUTE)

He laughs like a girl.
She laughs like a boy. Her grisly teeth,
she flirts heavily
dropping cigarette ashes to the floor.
I watch from this corner
slightly
leaning against this blue wall,
my knuckles whiter
than the white tissue paper
I am squeezing.
I brought flowers, clutching
these scrawny stems; they stink
now like dirty rural dresses.
It is just that if he had known I was coming
and by all sensible means he should have,
this, then, was his own construction,
an enunciation for disorder.
I have flowers while he speaks to her
about blankets and drive-in movies.

Just watch me disappear perfectly.
She was promising him things, she
had unlimited funds. I have green palms,
three carnations, us both, tedious,
thirsty and available.
I have chills and fever.
Guess what age I should be when
I stroll back in, empty-handed
with a knife in my boot.

MAN IN BLUE AT CROSSROADS AT CITY PERIMETER

Isn't it always wrong Renardo,
forty-nine miles from home and comfortable
behind the wheel, the glinting, insufferable noonday
not a factor, the slippery contour of lake not a mirage,
but an antidote—still surfing, still sound, pure inculpable.
On the telephone they are connected: him undressed,
her undressed, on opposite city ends, baking.
The kitchen as illness, preponderantly his,
phone in one hand: the conduit.
In the other an emblem, a fixed meal: the confessed.
Catfish and tomato on white bread. Secretly, she must,
as you would, wonder if that invokes mayonnaise.
Smell of catfish on his fingers in such heat is a woozy hook.
Here he calls it an unpardonable act,
then emptily asks for forgiveness.
What would you call it?
Yes is yes.
No, child, no, mister, someone wants out, let someone out,
start searching for a sincere welcome, get on your hands
and knees because it is not easy, where it all
should be, preferably, with two ruby hearts of hope, on
target, in deep, and a million nights of mercury, going off.

WHY THE JUDGE'S CHAMBERS CAN CAN-CAN

You train your roaming eye
down to the undulation of his robe's hemline.
You're close enough to whiff a whisper of cinnamon breath.
His chambers are bright. Lots of double pane windows. Then an oddity—
framed, signed Dr. Seuss prints on the wall. Jim,
his assistant, lowly singing the hook from "Brickhouse,"
glances your way on *"lettin' it all hang out,"* a line lingered at. Glee
would be the word. With open hand the judge motions you
to sit. The comfortable invitee's
leather chair; sweet leather, milk chocolate color,
just enough sit and just enough give. The chambers' door
couldn't be wider open.

This judge feels like an ocean

as his sumptuous black robe is removed,
the familiar placing of it on the common coat rack.
It's unsuitable—the green cargo pants
and river sandals! Clearly he's a man,
this person who, with irenic mind, contours
behavior that binds other men.
At the lip of his gorgeous desk a polished
gold name plate. He jokes: touch it
and he'll send your prints for analysis. The way he says it
tells you he's cast it, his standard line. Whose nerves
are higher? You'd like to confound him, drive him
up his Seussian wall. He wants you to watch him
in these chambers, know he's requested
your company. But he has a big kindness, a titanic
love for whomever he loves, and river
sandals are shoes for him, not a statement.

Without your asking

his assistant presents a beautiful glass of cold water.
You appreciate this. Liquid
sentence that makes you
change your unjourneyed mind.

GEOMETRY FOR INTERMEDIATES

Greetings from Williamsburg, VA:
rays of sunlight filter prettily
through the plantation
shutters. The servants look
distinctly
like the privileged
family they work for.

Taciturn cowboy: his kingdom
for a mule. Hard being married
to a bronc rider like that. He says five
words all night and ten of them she can't
make out. Mule circles leg-heavy and
lazy toward the hay truck
but goes further and has no ego. Mules rule.

Family court judge approaches an
accident in the intersection: "One of the silly
things that's going to be happening is
you are going to be separating out your money
and you will begin feeling that pain shortly. Kids,
you don't go to Six Flags because
the old man didn't pay child support."

Says the buxom lass
to the maestro of this body's
desire: pony up. Heels down,
squeeze the inner thighs.
But not so much as to alarm the animal.
Cover this, this, this
and that big old thing with ivies
and pink peonies. Back in
to the point of apex.

CINCINNATI BACON

This one man is more than the usual man.

>   *No man can be more than the usual man.*

This one man is more.

>   *Impossible. No man is more than another.*
>   *A man may have more, he may know more,*
>   *he may do more, but he is not more than another.*

This one man alone, I tell you, is more.

>   *How is he so special?*
>   *Can he wear two pair of shoes at the same time?*

This man can wear two pair of shoes
at the same time.

>   *How, has he two pair of feet?*
>   *Is he a deviant of nature?*

This man is special.

>   *There is no such thing.*
>   *Not at the bottom. Not to God.*

He wears galoshes.

>   *Numbskull! Cosmetic trickery!*
>   *How is the man particular?*

He responds not to kindness, nor beauty, nor love.

>   *Not at all? Not ever? Not love?*

Never. Only to horses.

>   *It speaks for itself:*
>   *You don't respond? You're unresponsive.*

ANTS: THE TRUER STORY

Look to the ant, thou sluggard
Consider his ways, and be wise.

PROVERBS 6:6

Earth, grass, trees, competitor bugs (not your best
friends), but somehow nothing jazzes you like the interior
of my house. Your boss's directive: Scouts! Find pie!, and you
jostle the baseboard perimeters, on a luxurious guess safety will out.
Little but faith moves your serpentine, occasionally fruitless trails,
what moves you, when perchance here might be it, the dog's bowl
well worth your trouble, a kind of chow muscatel.
You used to be lovely; lovely, mediocre bugs.
So who precisely was I to think to stand
in my own yard in my bare feet on a late spring day?
Converged scarcely describes it; by the dozens you nipped,
you bit my ankles: Gotcha lady, gotcha good, now scram,
we're moving here—well! This is my house, that is my grass
and I will stride across it wide-legged and barefoot—only to broadcast
the mighty ant bait like piñata candy raining down on children's heads,
the ant bait like grated Parmesan, like mini-bombs, I
cannot throw enough to satisfy my fear, then one of you
attacks a tiny morsel straightaway, when one is all it takes,
soon sixty of you, seventy, are lying on it, feasting, in
ant delirium. The yellow bait is black with ants, and me
in heaven. Soon comes that nervous system dance of death
you shake like castanets, shimmying
the lights out, hyperbolic ant spirals in the dirt and grass.
It is not because I want to
but I must kill you, all that I
am not. You work as if there is no tomorrow
and rarely panic, the hours long, tediously long, the
sharing of food, you do not improvise or complain,
you tolerate each other. You sleep in heaps.
And back of each of you are hundreds.

My husband says I cannot kill you all, but he
was not bothered by your party in the cupboards.
His teeth did not set after you breezily
ate through the pancake mix box and this, after
you jimmied through the concrete foundation of my
sweet home. What *is* that? I say do not
come twining that merengue line across the pavement
onto my property, upon my doormat, because destroy you I will,
and so this, in grief, I too concede—your queen is a jealous queen,
her plan without a plan, a forbearance.

PLED

Your client's deposition, and an omission
never revealed has jaggedly surfaced. Now
the conference room's walls buckle and duck,
halving themselves like the taking of sides
in a schoolyard fight. The defense attorney is so joyous
she frowns bitterly as masquerade. You fume
gaseous, the calculated implosion, the knowing
toying, another's bonanza. As though
you just learned you'd been switched at birth.
After hours you school your client—dumpsters
in backlots containing company garbage
contain company property—yet,
he only thinks he's stolen.

Everyone recalls the pageant of your activist wife,
her unperfumed huff, delivering your dinner
to the office. She spoke to no one, tossed the hot
frozen dinner tray atop your desk, other people's problems
on paper beneath the dripping gravy, her statement made.
The day you know the instant case is all but lost
she files her own petition.

When night comes, night itself turning
its back at one long confederacy,
you roam through thick blue and gray texts,
seeking the song of law where it levels,
raking out not the answer but the match,
every page you turn returns your argument to you
as your own countenance weathers like the desert hills,
as if you were shepardizing the laws of Moses,
where all is sound, the elements menacing
and the faintest bereft wail is a chime of enunciation.

HAND ME THOSE GLOVES

In America, land of loving
to pile on plenty of rules, the powers that be
have okay'd three features
for patents—New! Useful!
Nonobvious!—so you can now holler out
it was you who fashioned something
    no other man can call his.

~

The dusty breeze has age in it
and swishes the yellowy-green eucalyptus leaves
like a fondling. You finally appreciate wind, hear
it warble through those dagger-shaped leaves.
It reminds you of the longing to caress
    the back of someone's gladiator neck.

The Casa Grande Ruins, bookended by two
seasons, no more: Summer's days into nights, long, hot and
hard, but the desert is your home. Winter's nights,
frigid compared, churlish,
    but the relief exquisite.

Industrious, how every single year
the roses seem nonchalant
to the skullduggery buzzing about them.
Why is a good question, yet not the red, the pink, the
yellow are fancied. Think on the white spider,
frank as milk, making its home
in the dizzying petals
of the white Kennedy rose.
Poised there in artificial recline, knitting
its meticulous sweaters of
    come to me.

THE LANTERN

There is this old man, accustomed to driving up and down
a very big hill to work, placing calls on a small phone
the whole distance because he is always lonely. You he calls

when he's heading away, inferring:
so long, you can't catch me, guess my pleasure.
He is not good-looking as he thinks.

He sends nude pictures of himself over the internet.
He dreams of apple trees, the apples ripening to green.
An open gate can't help its own downward self.

Why not instead say, "Ladies, I'm flattered
you show involvement but the vigor's not there anymore,
whirling these balls in the air, and some of you

have husbands. I enjoy too much my wrinkly white ass
to acquire intimate acquaintance with buckshot." That said, just
go. Steer your slapdash symbolic driftboat back to firm symbolic land.

There a lantern will illumine you, the common one, your own offing,
infused with mistake, bemusement. Does he not know what it takes
a woman to prepare her mind to have an affair properly?

In the old parable, four calico felines lie gasping, pink shreds of meat
on the flat plate, then a voice, "Feast yourselves, on me." This new parable
props an old voice, "Here's five dollars, buy that cola you wanted."

Ditch that manure. Turn to the page before last. See the handsome woman
remain elegant as she crumples the bill back into his bloated palm,
tears welling but not falling, *don't do this,*

because the full sculptured moon above and the stars surrounding
would like you to know purity can be bestial,
even so, do not now or ever wash your hands of this.

DESERT BIRD

I am out in this desert nine years now, and I suffer
for the cold steely rain of other birds' days. I,
a desert bird; not kin to the orange-breasted
conspicuous robin who industriously abides
the downpour for the plump, pinkish worms to unearth
prone on the walk, like delicacies adrift off a shipwreck;
nor to the crafty, aping blue jay, who, stringing a predator,
descends screaming; nor the blood red cardinal, skilled operatic,
who against whitest snow, stops the breath
from his perfect beauty. I, the bird exiled; the soup pot holds
no cup of broth for me. In this blistering land no melody
betrays my post, my song squeaks and creaks, my bill
less a bill than a pincer, and so, pathetically, I covet.
Come dusk, why I put up a racket is at last
I know the sun is a nettle who will tool me to its whims,
water is first and last, shade the sustainer, and shiny
black bees, big as a man's thumb, beckon me through the holes
in woody things to desert greenery spiked with fangs.
The cutting thorns and blades mark my body's borders.
Sparse blossoms of color, vigilantly reared; artless blooms
but fiercely policed. When life feels a mutiny
I fly to the water I think I see.
I will continue to die for it.

POST-AUTOPSY: OR, CAN I TAKE JUST THIS WITH ME?

Preface: For conversation's sake, why not say a book
started it, though the truth is somewhere
in the middle. In all history, when, I ask you, has a book
started anything? It was a man started it, the book confiscated
from his office, pages dog-eared brown
but heavy like steel. Loaned on the promise it would be
returned. Photos peppered the text: the badly mangled,
met-their-end-poorly, brutally deceased. His own curiosity peaked
when under tangerine silk he noticed the
articulated curves of my sexual hips. Big men prefer
a politic access. The enjoyment of two-way clearance.
The book he lifted like a speck. Deciphered every impenetrable
nonnegotiable word. And wasn't it *so* him, and I, exposed
to the infantile restlessness of the overaccomplished, jerked
over his repeated glancing toward the door, the sore
act of deleting diminutive secret symbols
off a wee metal phone. But oh, then he palmed my pussy
with the decelerated stroking knowing hand
of doctor lust. And I cried do do it.
Just enlighten me how it traverses from her to there, here to
there, him to her.

Photo 2-1. Male. The toilet as death seat.
Limbs splayed in ugly directions. Head wedged
between toilet tank and beadboard wall. Downward bevel
of the mirror catches the reflection of saturated pajamas,
beautiful wasted plum silk. The heartbreaking cream
stripe down the side of each pajama leg. Why he feuded
with whoever sought him to such a degree that
that person extracted a gun from their jacket, the one
deliberate bullet, and what kind of fray could lead to such
a brilliant final plummet, what matter now? Conjecture,
the book would insinuate, is the mother of investigation.

Shot downstairs, he retreated upward to the bathroom
seeking safety and porcelain. Where the water is.
Water, then the drains.

Aside, Adults Only: Did I mention women love a man
who everyone in the room listens to because he *is*
the information? I fill my mouth up with him, when
I tongue that tender soulful ridge in circles, let the pre-come
slip out the corner of my mouth, my eyes on his eyes,
isn't it I answering all the crucial questions
at the big industry convention? *Who's not getting a load*
of this? Anyone need a memo? Ain't this happy
like it ought to be?

Photo 2-4. Female. Ticked off as a ten-minute
intermission between the acts of assorted men's lives.
A knock at the door and the leaden arms
of an ardent suitor tentacled around. As best
she could she fell and fell away. He thrashed
her interior until, like a rose, she was ruby red
and becoming. Split in two at
the genitals like a deseeded melon. Silk stockings,
a second skin peeled in shards down to her calves.
Her peep-toed shoes still on, and the pretty gold hat.

Author's Note: Gentlepeople: Assembly disperses as a tide.
The dead slip away to their unearthed gone. What is not
to love about the hold-on-a-minute *maybe* of it all?
Who can't afford to dance like there's no tomorrow,
to lounge upon the silk sheets of a promise
below the constant breeze.
The old book, it never was returned.
To waver, to waver, to waver, this hoary
human thing.

III

PASSOVER

Finally: after the battered, powerful red-and-white crane,
operated by a man called Maverick, whose huge hand
I personally shook, was raised seven stories high to the top
of Mayo Hospital, dangling steel beams like matchsticks
but scrupulously set on the roof to install higher space,
making room for even more of the unwell and terribly needy,

the sodomite prostate,
its ruffled capsule battered by voracious cancer
but not burst, and not spread to the thirsty lymph system,
had been yanked like a satanic thing out of there. By spidery robot arms.

The M.D. Ph.D. surgeon operated half a room away, fiddling
a joystick in front of a screen to burn death out of the trunk
of my husband. Yet his hands were small as a girl's, the fingertips
tapered down like candelabra fine-drip wax. Earlier, he'd carried
a backpack to Pre-op like a high school kid on his way to first period.

Doctor doctor, I prayed and held my breath. When a terrible storm blew in
a nurse hovered over my husband, said to the medical team, *If the electricity goes*
I tell you that wife will be barreling through those operating room doors.
Doctor doctor, whom I could crush with one passionate hug…

five hours later he entered the little consult room
to tell me the surgery couldn't have gone better. I swore
at the cancer, at the prostate, who we'd nicknamed Ernie,
Ernie the bad seed, and I made him tell me
three times how it had not spread, the nerves intact,

and I believed I would be able to make love to my husband again,
because he was there, alive, and his beautiful penis
might know erection once more, because I was selfish, and torn;
death had passed over this one day
our very house. I kissed the right hand of our surgeon

as if he embodied some mythical conception, the finite hand
that processed medicine and technology through the belly
of a simple man so that he could come home, and I

granted the privilege to shut the widow's door, an empty room
with only a straight-back chair. The doctor then was up out of his seat,
would stay no longer, someone else was under anesthesia.
That person required attending.

CAMPING TIPS FOR SINGLES

You finally meet someone who compliments
your idea of interesting and he or she invites you
to do something entirely out of your element.
Do not regurgitate your recent meal, freeze
up in place or prevaricate. Try it,
try it for the sake of your ancestors
who tried everything: the shaky wooden ladder
above the many colorations of soil, the shorn pelt,
the hand extended speechless towards another hand.

Blame is a date-stopper, a useless commodity.
Yes, the metal coffeepot and granola bar wrappers
left outside the tent are big mistakes.
And yes, the real interrogatory always boils down to:
How much *can* a mountain lion smell?
For there it is, the snuffling, the padded-toe ambulation,
the making of indistinct but purposeful soft sounds
far enough away from the tent
neither of you is shrieking.
The creature's nocturnal precision. Remember
the value of not bumping into anything; it crosses
the species gap. This is why
the good date always pockets hurricane matches.
Nothing like a roaring fire to scare a catamount
back onto its sward.

The compelling date is observant, yet encumbered.
No one can parallel your inimitable style
so do benevolence. Witness the marring of the sun's
surface, those orphic patterns not unlike
the deciphering of tea leaves at the palm reader's
but on a gigantic scale the size of which
you could get alarmed by, but don't. Sunspots.
An imperceptible little shade today, granted;

tomorrow, a mountain of tidal stoppage.
When and if you return to your daily lives
think upon that monstrous beetle you prodded
with a dead branch. Waddling its girth away
from your amusement, its bizarre frontal pincers
dragging, and when it decided for you that you were
done with it, it lifted its immense household
off the ground and flew.

INTIMATIONS FROM UNDER THE GREAT BEAR

Didn't we have a time, that soft and sumptuous night,
high up on the craggy cliffs, the six of us, the small
kindling fire we struggled to keep ablaze, we clustered
together for warmth, and told the same shared stories with even
more pronouncement, the banter, the laughter, it was something.

Old friends know in profile what strangers require
a novel's length to discern. Whatever it is
that says we part, sends us down peculiar avenues
to distant vistas. In the leaving we mourn longevity; upon
arrival the commotion belongs to us, elegant, promising, new.

Take the length of rope, the mittens, the beacon of light.
The summer's hot winds are nearly behind us. Forgive
and forgive the tangential mockeries we have thrust
upon ourselves. The last things to take are always the
most engaged. Why, yes, take this; turn it up, and over, and under.

We named the starry constellations and created others
where knowledge failed us. There we saw two friends
holding hands or the sail of a ship in full wind. That night
we waited like pilgrims for the light to rise and throw itself
upon the lenient sky. We agreed it came wondrously well, the sun.

THE DRY CLEANER'S DAUGHTER

The dry cleaning business had its own mythologies. My Jewish
father, unceremoniously, called his Viking Cleaners.
Perhaps he forged himself the plundering marauder
of Devon Avenue, where stood Selma's delicatessen,
Mlodinoff's photography studios, and the pastry-luring
Gitel's bakery; all quaked from the reverberating wake
of his landship station wagon, its suspension sprung, wheezing
and harrumphing along the potholed road, its interior stuffed
with bundles of the *kehillah's* soiled ensembles of finery.
Great care readied the clothes for cleaning. Buttons,
shrouded with satiny cloth, zippers zipped and waxed, hooks
detached to safeguard gossamer fabrics from vicious snags.
Next, the pockets, reviewed—and there, from the sundry folds
of faceless pockets, sometimes my father extracted intricate filigreed gold
mezzuzot, and forthright silver Stars of David, and one exceptional piece,
brushed brass, in the shape of the holy tablets, encrusted
with striking Judaic stones signifying commandments.
He reserved them in a cigar box a year or more.
No one remarked on or claimed their vanished valuables.
These he brought home to me, as offerings.

A brooding girl: where were people arriving at
or returning from that a sea engulfed them, seafoam
prickly in their lungs, and the choice was made not
to display their *mezzuzot* the entirety of the evening?
No one removes gold cuff links midway into an event.
No pearl cluster earrings wantonly set aside.
Anyone would inquire as to their whereabouts.
What coerced fine Jews to shed these symbols, place them
in outerwear's abundant depths and go on, blithely,
about their occasion? What amplified quality of
an evening had they? Did the company they kept, who
professed to care for them, care for them any more or less?
Was the wine spectacularly replenished, the dance

simply one degree more rousing?
The Christian does not remove the cross and stealth it away
in trouser or skirt pockets. A likeness of
the young Jewish journeyman is proudly displayed
around the neck. The crosses are large.

I now know my father drove that wagon
for his family's sake. From out its windows wafted
premonitions and resignations in brocades of gray
cigar smoke. I was seven when I discovered Jesus Christ
and his mother were Jews. I confess I
was confused. I surmised he'd grown up the same
old way, the kids he'd hung out with, cousins, siblings, the
whole citizen block, families squabbling, embracing. He knew,
but any Jewish child knows the riotous arousal
they simply walked in on. Options were afforded him.
Would he, elocutionistic, peripatetic, charged and emitting,
with his Jewish buddies in tow, have removed all vestiges
of Jewish ornamentation, as he wound
his way up and over, on the road to Capernaum?
And in his travels, if he stooped
at the dusty roadside to hand a darkhaired
girl some cloth from his family tree, she
would have needed nothing of instruction, less
of intervention, and deliverance but an anathema.
It was a given, a corolla of nimbus,
a thing to be held onto in its immoderate beauty.

PORTRAIT OF THE TWO OF YOU, FESTOONED

Behold the quixotic sesame seed
miniature of surprising versatility,
its red, black or sweetish-ivory jacket.
What fortune's first son stood energized
sufficient to capture its winning nuttiness?
Huge the staunch hope must have been that it
prove bargainable, or possibly edible and actually fruitful.
Crux of my feeling for you is that procession. Come back
to the desert and its searing thanklessness
which undisguised you, reduced the rest of us
to acquit you harmless. This inability to keep a simple
engagement took years of practice. The caustic penmanship
nothing but a blanket of need to be held. *See you laugh in a photograph,*
that's all I ever wanted to do, sang the Irish poet, and he
with a greater vocabulary in wanderlust than I.
So thank you. Your exotic gifts, received intact from
the brown bandaged parcel, its olio of mysterious stamps.
The garland of carved stone petals
makes me feel like some reckless queen. The fez
is one jolly hat; I wear it unabashedly.
Thank you in the very way the train porter
disembarks from the train car steps
setting the stepbox
below the stair. Visualize
the journey back as understatement in ice, woods, prairie.
A ring of one skeleton key proves any door compliant.
Turn; come. Say farewell
to that humid green shoretown preposterous
with vegetation. As I speak,
rapier hawks sail twenty stories high, full-winged
on blooming thermals of shelf air,
shell glints off the dry
mountain face like a
beckoning from a lighthouse summit.

MOB DAD

—for M.L., in memoriam

The mob father schooled his daughter, my best friend,
the year we were seventeen, *Girls, never leave a paper trail,*
me in the background, and then gave each of us two one-hundred
dollar bills, told us to go buy something, and
do not make it practical. Back when you
could shop in the old neighborhood; nice boutique
stores like *One-Way Ticket* or *Ruby's Blue Sleeves.*
Life was good in the pizza
business. What he meant was girls have it
harder than boys in the most insidious, thin-skinned ways, so
we should try our best not to regret
or implicate ourselves, a brainstorm we only really
figured out two decades later. Which was of course
way too late, the blueprints wrought, and for her, the end abruptly,
vault sealed—and who doesn't pray for the soul of an old friend's life,
lodged perilously upon the ice-encrusted brink, pray
that it idle in the bosom of mercy.
Once in her true youth, her father tacked the first
orphan notice upon her head: that no man would
want her but for his money.
What it did was make her hungry for the things hundred dollar bills
buy. And pizza. The hunger for that knee-trembling pizza.
And full-size whole turtle pies. And lousy men
with limousine-length egos. And gold, and gold only,
because silver you have to rub and rub to keep pretty.

KAFKA CAN DO

We crowd around the pantry, diplomatically
drinking bad morning coffee. Mother Suite's private blend.
At first her declaration is such that we wonder
we hear it first. Brainstorms
will perform a cakewalk across the linoleum floor.
Our treat. His latest knock-kneed triumph,
which he demonstrates with surprising professionalism.
Brainstorms' kudo: a squeeze Kafka doll
for play in the bathtub.

At lunchtime, Brainstorms sits in his highchair
dictating strained peas and orders.
He pokes his Kafka and weans proper
easy variations on everyman's double-shot
and he petitions, as Mother Suite spoons,
coaxes airplane trails
to his lips: "Carry me curled embryonic,
blessedly over this mad waning labyrinth."
Mother confides to those of us still here,
he simply means he wets his bed.

A handful of us keeps on and by evening
the message is simple. Whoever stole the grand prize
is requested to return it within the hour,
as Brainstorms' wrath
far exceeds the girdles of amateur thievery, promising
great bent connections at his disposal
even outside the confines of kitchen and toilet.
One of us whispers, "That perpetrating little wise guy,"—
Curtains. We all fall down as from something toxic.

TO THE CHIEF MEDICAL EXAMINER'S OFFICE

No one visits but for business.
You expect it to look like a morgue from the movies; instead, an
easement—this plain building. Ring the bell outside
in front of a locked door in front of a foyer
in front of a second locked door and finally to the Chief
Medical Examiner's office you go. Oil
and old fruit, faint aromas. The half-drunk
soda cans, the ugly desk, stacks of medical documents.
You glance at discolored letterhead, below it, outlined
anatomy figures, arrows pointed at dissected body parts,
the complicated Latin jargon written in a tight fist,
and you finger nothing.

He mouths bad or blue jokes, then sobers
to quiet the butterfly flush across your face. His
twinkly brown eyes, half-flirtatious. Is it you
he tweaks or you versus dead bodies all day long?
The Chief Medical Examiner pronounces *bilateral haemothorax*
    the very way
this morning you told your children the toast burned,
and while the rest of the world ends up at
pottery classes, investment seminars and line dancing,
he frequents the Weapons of Mass Destruction Workshop,
and the Fatal Blunt Head Injury Symposium; there, serious men
heed him. He tells them of the perfect dot
of pituitary in the brain, how like a grape it can be squashed between
thumb and forefinger, the tender matter plashed, casually, rid.

The Chief Medical Examiner has sunk his two hands
into nine thousand flesh bodies,
not one of whom would stir, come to, rise up—
and for a score of dead females,
found in the nest of their expired wombs
a tiny translucent baby or two together,
always the surprise of the finding,
as you surprise

to crack open one perfect speckled farm egg, only to behold
two viscous yolk orbs wobbling in the skillet.
The dumbfounded medley of surplus in death.

Alive two days ago, people
collect in the long hall they call the breezeway. Felons,
salesclerks, hoodlums, parents, all: misdemeanor homicides.
The murdered notables get private rooms, and curtains.
Fine bone china, more precious with the liquid drained
from them than if you brimmed with
gold bullion. And when are you the deviation?
When your murderer is a notable, or the gunshot
is not one to the gut, but one to the heart and fourteen to the groin.

What phantasm does he beckon when he retreats
to that home in the woods? His moonly wife
serves up her toothsome, smoking feast, as a nocturnal
but luminous craving creeps across his evening plate.
What airy morsel does he savor, let perch on his tongue
before he swallows? Softly
he reaches for his wife's elbow, to
bring the heat of her to him, a fragrant palace, the veiny foliage.

So under the sculptor's hands, the marble, too, has desire:
seething to be loosed from its casing, it keeps one eye aside.

To truss up a thick slice from a young man,
a cowboy from the Sonoran Desert, who belonged
to his black truck, his mother, and the great mountains Superstition,
and with wizardry make him whole, and songful,
to knot the thew to the horn of him,
witness him pick up his hat, his blade, his gloves
and his life and pass through the breezeway to
couple with the preoccupied immaculate day.
Unlassoed, unappeased, and happening in wavelengths of violet, green,
orange, red, and undulating
insensible light.
There are no words for it.

ALLOTMENT

Drafting a line on a napkin at a comedy club
or while on the phone with the pharmacy,
I steal time from my husband
like a junkie grabbing her drug.
And my husband has entertained reservations. He wants me
more wifely. I write
in the semi-dark. Dinner always simmers:
pork and curly kale, next night, steak and collards;
eating like country people.
I quick retreat to the bedroom, flop
on the bed to write these selfish lines by
the light of the hall sconce. He
will seek me out in a moment. Lucky.
Really, do I not
get that anyone would wish
for this in their right mind?

THE DAY JUDGE SPENCER LEARNED
THE POWER OF METAPHOR

Picture hangs crooked in jury room: crochet of buff-colored
haze sifts down into a market square. Someplace foreign
and difficult to get by in, with luggage for tables,
with uncaged chickens and strange grains.
Splotches of blue
        engage the eye: produce, trinkets, jars
for consideration; the changing
of azure hands.

                            The judge
wants two things for his day to be bazaar.
Accord, and proper procedure wrapped round it.
The sleepy, overbooked judge
ensconced in a procedural throw. So the proceedings
can step up.
           A jury
wants one thing if plucked from the pool. Confetti
and lots of it, with gashes, stitches and strangulating
purse handles. Juries called to civil matters are bummed—
who wants to root five days exposed
to promissory taffy, and its severance
upon the back of a lumbering, citified beast?
The good civil lawyer makes a robbery
of the process. As if doing you the favor.
        In comes the lady
     attorney for plaintiff.
Her face is classically round, pointless, yet the courthouse
bathroom's porcelain sink rests enshrined
with unlovely residual vomit. The
disgruntled employee she champions
has his own fears. How did it get this far? What's
not to like about his new job? How many vacation days
had he now for the family, the holidays?
         At table opposite, the defense attorney's

own client is absent. Fluke,
                and not without consonance. Top
of her lungs, the lady's opening statement
opening line, she shrieks, "Fucking prick moron!"
and she's off, stomping. If you saw her
you might say what an actress, stellar performance,
and she would say she hobbled around
on bloody stumps, cut off at the knees.
                Her star exhibit:
                                incendiary memo
full of bullying invective,
                each handwritten line
                                rising jagged off the page
flying like bats unstuck, and furious.
                                The lady pounces, preens
at the box of people—the robbery. Midway
between table and box she stops, small
run at the heel of her dark hose. Her figure
aligns with the judge on his perch,
        behind him scalloped eggshell lighting
                across the stern cubist walls of the room.
                Up above, brown grid of a ceiling.
The light deepens to oyster against the brown.
She lets her insides drift some.
        Judge Spencer eyes the emergency
color wheel taped to his desktop. He
pulls up stakes: jury—bailiffed back to its room.
Man in gallery, quit drinking that grape soda. Mind
the dignity of this shop.
                        O weatherman, hear tell
        there's a gale of motions on the air...
The defense attorney flails the three-headed D's,
Dismiss, Dismiss, and Direct your verdict
on this mess for god's sake. The lady attorney
says all she wants is recess, then mispronounces
the defense attorney's name four times
on record on purpose. Judge Spencer sees

trout fishing on the horizon; hooks and lures
packed in his neat tackle box. "Madam, your craziness
becomes you," and because he is backlit
and elevated, and because the jury
has been excused from this exchange, she reaches
into the black bag behind her—
     because she's Doll Anonymous,
she should be hammocking in Cozumel, sipping
a peacock-blue cocktail, rich orchid behind her ear,
as something approaches, low-slung, strewing
greetings on the unpaved road—
    ' "No recess, proceed. Bailiff, bring 'em in."
      and upon the vacant
plaintiff's table, which should be stacked with legal pads,
deposition transcripts, manicured accordion files, she deposits
    a favor, one single regulation baseball,
   white with red stitching, unscuffed.
  The way it rolls a little and wobbles—
    to the bewilderment of the reentered jury—
every time the table is thumped, which is often,
the empty table with nothing
but the ball on it,
the whole episode buzzing, behind her
   the thing virtually throbs.
      Moment of outmaneuver.
Suited, oiled, the defense attorney queries his first witness
to man up. But get a load of the lady! Sidling right
   into mid-court, she's queued, arm's length
from defense at the lectern.
The case way out in the grass sits, atop the memo.
White baseball gleams. Syzygy.
     Judge Spencer's eyes narrow
in complot, acres of ink. Yet he breathes pacific. The feeling is soil
but where to put his finger to it? She'd process
explicit directives inside a hair's breadth,
address defense counsel's mount of objections
by the boot of her hip. Time

                    wasn't earmarked
for the encroachment of men. Impervious,
standing there, as if she'd caught sight
    of a beveled mirror and a set of sky-high orbs
        like a dream, and still an indisputable radiance
            proceeds from outside her, in nature, like so.
                            And so to Judge Spencer's
vision of a solitary white rowboat at dusk. Gray-blue
backwoods summer lake. Birds flown to the leafy beds
of the treetops. The only stirring, a faint cupping and rocking
of the vessel, as if some great freight
had been pitched from its wooden side. Comes
then the hymnlike pearling down of moonshine—
every single thing is relevant under its misapprehended pull.

DEER

Late fall in its insufficient overcoat.
The man in fall at a serene clearing.
He found pacific places a kind
of stammering. When time came,
the taking of an animal purely for food
meant successful aim
and provision. Years of denying
himself the ripe, unaggressive lover
turned his hunting skills
to art. Somewhere in his cabin,
a journal filled with one line repeatedly,
this wanting you is torment.
Yet his sense for where living
things would be
next
was resplendent.

In the wet woods, slick gummy leaves,
chestnut-colored, fragrant mud.
Heavy and light, penetrating
and airy, *run from here, a place
is not a safe place with this sort*,
the killing arrows suggested. The
brittle wind, advancing through, risked
life is dependent on actual use.
In the tops of the trees
the garrulous birds concurred,
while the creatures of gravity
knew torsion.

THE PERSIMMON CAN SEE YOU

When you're a lawman and you're dealing with people
it's better to go not so much by the book but by the heart.
      —Barney Fife
      The Andy Griffith Show

The persimmons are very ripe and finally edible.
In a blue glass bowl they nest at judge's elbow.
Two semi-hostile, soon-to-be ex-spouses await words
from judge's mouth. The meat of the fruit
is lush in its heaviness, seems loath to relinquish
itself for the sustenance of others. The people bristle.

Judge raises the thickest persimmon, tells the couple his
popular story: the snorting rodeo bronc, standing upright
for life, its one deftly placed hind-kick—the beast's delicate
eyelashes promise the shocking kick will concuss a man
into the unpredictable hereafter—the coffin bone
in its hoof guarantees as much.
Judge declares *bad* that each secretly thieves and
openly covets the other person's things. The persimmon is twisted
this way and that. Each spouse spins abruptly angelic.
He caresses the fruit, comparing their homemade
disasters to the horse, valiantly
if misleadingly penned, roped so gingerly
by the scruff of the neck. In the gallery,
those relatives or friends or new significant others,
anyone with any nickeling anecdote will get to speak,
that they not depart with the mistaken notion
if only he'd heard their one mindblowing
contribution, all the difference
would have been made to the world and their relation.
But the couple: He invites them—because it's his
to allow—permission—to get up on it, except they are,
and honestly, who isn't, wary of permission. *I'm being asked,*

he says, t*o be arbitrary under the guise*
of being asked to be equitable. Best I can do is separate
the two of you with a few pieces of paper. This is his
pronouncement. He is deathly quiet afterward.
If they knew him they'd know he is most
dangerous now. Most questionable. But *permission*:

It's an invitation. Get up on it, sling your slappy-ass feet
through the stirrups. Ride out your bruised lives, your bruised
improvable lives to within a quarter-inch of saddle broke.
Nearby, the persimmons announce: their bouquet alone
beautifies the proceedings.
And that's the kind of thing people remember.

BELVEDERE

What's left to conjure your precise philosophy? You said
words themselves conduced—through one great
empyreal monocle they view us while we use them.
Wield their talents at us like shop tools:
jagged hex sawing some bantam serendipity
in half, crosscut stratagem against the many bosses, polished
apple of perfidy or coy to cajole the girl to sit awhile. You
saluted the pedigree of language, *the apple doesn't fall far,*
then cultivated an orchestra of grunts and hoots. Hawking said
once the universe was nothingness, was perfect
but unstable. Its compulsion to eventually be
ultimately felled the likes of you. You got
the death you asked for. Vast fear attached:
which when pondered proves endearing
for in the end you actually were human,
the black space wheeled into bore
nothing of the comfort of a grandfather's
afghan worn proudly about.

At the last you turned
metaphors of ships and shoreline.

For others you were a piece of a house.
The vestibule. No mere perfunctory berth
to hang one's hat or place the misted
umbrella in its stand. The vestibule's
true calling is its purpose: to lead us elsewhere within.
And to still have not touched bottom. Oh, but the gushing leaves
a literary mess. And so the final book on your nightstand spoke
of an interleaving—whose meaning cut, addled, becharmed
the simple terms: being, and belonging as in, *you wouldn't
marry me, would you,* and then washed away frothy, adrift
even as we entreat such fine filaments, no handhold anywhere,
your point exactly. Bring on a tin roof and slatwood floor

to sound the fey code of the denizens' ticking heels.
Here's to clement days. You are had now in the way
of the legitimately unfathomable
but with a brace of fragrance,   *mirabile dictu*

POST-AUTOPSY: OR, ALL THOSE CELL PHONES ATTACHED TO YOUR BELT LOOK LIKE GRENADES

And so now, somewhere, someone is singing.
A man's ragged voice, but full, with incredibly
tender edging to it. The kind of man a
serious woman takes to a wet bed. I might blame it
on a marvelous night of soft rain
in a tucked-away garden. Or how his hands, like hovercraft,
ease upon me weightless. Or that a cool mist
films his entire pale body, and I suck at it. The knot of his nipple
hard and undefended under my pink pink tongue.
His large arms, jaws around my waist. I am
tired of wishing. The embrace is anaconda;
constriction as his want stiffens.
I wonder if a thoughtful reader approached this
brackish thing, would only one question be lashed
and uttered: what is it with hunger? Incomputable effort and time
spent deferring to it, and its guises. A mere vocabulary
of coins to measure it. Meanwhile,
the appointed wait on determinations
of great significance. Letters
slide back and forth between offices. Many mad
waiting. Some in grief. Some anxious on calculated returns.
By tomorrow afternoon, the clear jar of formaldehyde, in it
snippets of organs bobbing, will make its way to a crisp
many-windowed room. Look closer,—
I have to go away from this
before I cannot get away. Only to find out
vitally I am nothing special.
—a mean burr straddles the top of the microtome.
Hoo wee! No one can read a slide this choppy.
Is there anyone in the entire
building who can make sense
out of this slide.

ON THE MIND SUMMITING IN A POOL OF SWEAT

Not sunup yet, but that same caliber of gray
as dusk on its way toward dark
except there are bits of cream dropped in it, and the kitchen
is strange, in this light like night but not. Coffee
would percolate me if the kettle would appear. Because
darned if I don't see a thing outlandish I'm afraid to say.
Outside corner of the backyard there, a scrawny
silhouette of a small man, he darts, jabs
as a sparrow caught in the rafters
aspires to blue sky. I've just moved into this house, I
do not know it; my mail delivery isn't flowing yet.
Some thirty years, widowed, retired, my real house
gone, and here I am. Perhaps the landscapers
didn't yet get their last invoice paid up
and a cease service note from the prior owner.
After all, he might be about to fertilize something—but where's
his edging equipment, the bags of manure, a shovel—

And he approaches; sidewinder. My glass arcadia door.
A decorative garden rock, helmet
clutched to his breast. If he admires it
I could gift it to him. Some people possess queer
penchants for decorative rocks. Whatever I do, I do
not run. This will infuse him with courage,
and game. Running prey can be delicious.
I might holler through the as-yet-unbroken glass,
I too have a gun. And I do, which I do
not, and which he does not, although he too hollers it,
which of course I do not know yet for certain. And now
a new idea is knocking, except he is demanding
where is my car? And I say I didn't say I
have a car, why do you think I
have a car, what are you talking about, car...

As if this is philosophy class and I am a babe
and shining again for the sexy professor
from New York City, his tight black pants and sharp
black shoes, long wicked hair, two black eyes,
and hammered gold
wedding band worn knuckle to knuckle
on the third finger of his right hand, like
an exclamation against gullibility. Him
in whom I possessed a slobbering crush, oh
to exhibit debatable powers
of deductive reasoning rather
than be a goat to a crime scene and I
at the helm of it and if not helm, certainly
first goddamn mate, nautically speaking,

but like a bag of wind, I digress. Seems
the two skittish mahogany Doberman pinschers,
who sleep deeply as if pill-addicted,
now groggily navigating the kitchen table's legs
for the metal chink of the breakfast bowl, stir me,
the idea widens into a cauldron,
my mind enters as a tugboat, ugly, ill-starred
and perspiring, but all engine
into this moment of my life mine and not mine
for I want my soul to persist in my body
and I want the skies to hail down whatever they please
but upon me too, and when tomorrow brings
its eleventh-hour appreciation
in a classic frock, I want to attend
with the fanfare of the unrecognized, the barely-by, fully-
grown, touring the uproarious strains of what love sounds
like to the living.

CYNTHIA SCHWARTZBERG EDLOW holds an MA with a specialty in Poetry from the University of Illinois at Chicago. A Pushcart Prize nominee, her work has appeared widely in numerous journals and anthologies, including *The American Poetry Review, Arizona Attorney Magazine, Barrow Street, Cimarron Review, Gulf Coast, Smartish Pace*, and *The Tusculum Review*. A recipient of the Willow Review Prize for Poetry, a Beullah Rose Poetry Prize, and an award from the Chester H. Jones Foundation National Poetry Competition, her poems have also been featured in the anthologies *Not A Muse* (Haven Books), *In the Eye* (Thunder Rain Publishers), and *The Emily Dickinson Awards Anthology* (Universities West Press). She lives in Gilbert, Arizona.